Published by Macdonald Children's Books
Simon and Schuster International Group
Wolsey House, Wolsey Road
Hemel Hempstead HP2 4SS

First published in Great Britain by
Macdonald Children's Books 1989

Text copyright © 1989 Nicholas Fisk
Illustrations copyright © 1989 Caroline Crossland

*All rights reserved*

Photoset in 16 pt Garamond by Goodfellow & Egan
Colour origination by Scantrans Pte Ltd, Singapore

Printed and bound in Belgium by
Proost International Book Production

BRITISH LIBRARY CATALOGUING IN PUBLICATION DATA
Fisk, Nicholas, *1923–*
  The telly is watching you
  I. Title  II. Crossland, Caroline
  823'.914 [J]

  ISBN 0–356–16802–6
  ISBN 0–356–16803–4 Pbk

Nicholas Fisk

# THE TELLY IS WATCHING YOU

Illustrated by Caroline Crossland

Macdonald Children's Books

# Chapter One

"Here's your orange drink," Ben said to Shani. She was sitting on the carpet with her arms round her knees, looking snug. She smiled warmly up at Ben and took her mug of orange.

This was the best part of their day. School was over. Now was the time to drink orange, eat cake and watch the telly. Lovely.

"And here's your cake," Ben said. He had cut a huge slice for her – just as big as his own, because they were best friends.

"Good old telly," he said.

He sprawled beside Shani and pressed the little buttons on the TV's remote control. He and Shani called it the Blopper.

The TV screen lit up warmly, almost as if glad to be watched.

Shani wriggled about on the carpet. She did not like the programme.

"Try another channel," she said, through a mouthful of cake. "This is awful."

When she said this, the TV screen glowed a little less brightly, as if disappointed.

Ben blopped the Blopper. Now the screen showed horse-racing.

"Boring!" said Shani.

"No, wait a mo, let me see who wins," said Ben.

"Rotten old *horses*," said Shani. "Who needs them?"

They forgot the telly to have a quarrel.

Ben said, "You always want things your way!"

And Shani sang "Boring, boring, boring!"

The screen went dimmer and dimmer, almost as if it were sad to be ignored.

But then it gave a sudden *flash!* – a flash so bright that Ben and Shani just had to look.

"Boring, am I?" the telly said to itself. "I'll show them . . ."

Because this telly was different. All TV sets are clever machines. But this one was cleverer than any other.

People could watch *it*, of course . . . But this TV could watch *people!* And think thoughts!

## Chapter Two

Now the TV screen showed the racecourse crowds. The cameras went from person to person.

"Look!" Shani gasped. "That was me! I just saw *me!* I can't believe it!"

"Impossible," Ben said, and reached for the Blopper.

Before he could use it, the telly changed channels all by itself!

"I don't understand these humans," the telly said to itself. "But I think . . . if I try . . . I can show these two something they will really like!"

The screen showed a nature programme. A man and a woman, both in sweaters and gumboots, talked about fieldmice. The camera moved in to show a close-up of a pretty little mouse with bright eyes and twinkling whiskers.

The mouse was held cupped in a hand. Not the man's hand. Or the woman's. The hand of a young girl, a brown hand . . .

And a young girl's voice said, "There, now! Who's a lovely mouse? Who's a little darling?"

"Me!" squeaked Shani. "That's me!"

Again Ben said, "Impossible!" Then he said, "Where am *I*?"

"Oh, somewhere in the background," Shani said. She was staring at the screen, nodding her head and smiling to encourage the telly to show more of her.

"Well, *she's* pleased with me!" the TV said to itself. "Though I can't think why. What's so special about being just a voice and picture in a box?"

Then it said "Ooops!" because it could not hold the picture any longer.

Now the nature programme was over and the screen was showing the news. "It was me, wasn't it?" Shani said. "I was actually on the telly! I was the star!"

"The mouse was the star, not you," Ben grumbled.

Shani did not hear him. "Was I good?" she said. "Do you think all the viewers liked me?"

"You were rotten," Ben said. "All girly-girly and cute." He was jealous, of course.

Shani took no notice. "Me, on TV!" she said. "Me, a TV star!"

Ben said "Grrr!" and pinched her slice of cake.

# Chapter Three

Soon, Shani and Ben appeared in all sorts of TV programmes. They found it quite easy to get on TV. You simply held the Blopper and wished. The telly did the rest.

"There!" the telly said to itself. It had managed to get them into a programme about a garden festival. "There you are, both of you! Waving to the cameras! I hope you're satisfied!"

But Shani and Ben were never satisfied.

For example, there was a programme about young motorbike rough-riders.

"Great!" said Ben, patting the Blopper. "Terrific! Bags I be the rider of that yellow bike!"

The rider of the yellow bike rode his machine along a narrow plank – up a waterfall – over a Volkswagen.

"Wow! Just my style!" said Ben.

"Huh!" said Shani. "That wasn't *you!* Look! There you are, scrunched up between those two men in anoraks! Just another spectator! Huh!"

"Grrr!" said Ben. He went out into the garden, slamming the door. He kicked a tree.

It hurt his toe.

The TV set was disappointed too.

"Goodness knows I try," it said, "but they don't realize how difficult it is. They want to be peakview. They want to be megastars. But I don't *arrange* programmes, I only show them. How ungrateful humans are! All the same . . ."

It went on thinking clever thoughts.

"Pop concert!" Shani said. "Brill!"

She blopped the Blopper and the screen showed rock stars and flashing lights and that smoke stuff and hundreds of raised arms, waving in time with the music.

"Where's *me*?" Shani yelled at the telly. "Why aren't I the star? This is my scene! Show *me!*"

The TV set tried so hard that it nearly blew a transistor. But however hard it tried . . .

"Oh, no!" Shani cried. She was there all right, on the screen. But not on stage, rocking away with the stars. No, she was just one of the arm-waving crowd. Ben stood beside her, not waving his arms, looking cross.

"If you're so clever," Shani said to the TV set, "*why can't you make me the star?*"

The TV set was worried. It was an upset set.

Of course, it could not reply to Shani – there was a programme on.

And it could not reply when it was switched off, because then it went silent.

All the same, it was a clever machine – cleverer than all the others. So it went on sorting through its circuits, trying to think of a plan . . .

# Chapter Four

Next day, after school, Shani was grumpy. "I don't want to watch telly," she said.

She just sat on the carpet picking at her cake crumbs.

"Oh, come on!" Ben said. "There's an animals programme after the announcements."

Shani muttered, "Don't care," and gloomily sipped her orange.

"Remember," said the TV announcer, "tomorrow, at this time, we'll be bringing you the *Royal Occasion!* The Queen will be opening the –"

Immediately, Shani came to life. "The Queen!" she said popping her eyes. "A Royal Occasion, with the Queen! Ooo, I can't wait!"

"There you are then," Ben said. "Something to look forward to."

But now Shani was talking to the TV set.

"Oh, *please,* nice, kind telly," she said, "that's what I want! To be on telly with the *Queen!* Please let me be there! Let me be the girl in a pretty frock who curtseys and gives the Queen her bouquet!"

Ben said, "If you're going to be the bouquet girl, bags I be the page standing behind the Queen holding a velvet cushion. And bags I wear a velvet hat and a red tunic with gold bits. And she hands her bouquet to me! And I take care of it for her!"

The TV set heard all this. "I'll do my best for you!" it said, making a silent promise. "I'll try, I really will. Because I'm getting to like the two of you. But it's going to be very difficult . . ."

It tried all sorts of things. In fact, it fiddled with its circuits so much that a fuse blew. Then the repair man had to come. His call cost pounds and pounds and Ben's father got in a temper.

# Chapter Five

The TV set was repaired and working perfectly the next afternoon, in time for the Royal Occasion.

Ben and Shani sat with eyes glued to the telly. "Perhaps this time," Shani whispered, "I'll really be there . . . as a star!"

Ben said "Grrr!" but he was just as hopeful and excited as Shani.

The Royal Occasion started. The Queen was there in a yellow hat with a ribbon. And all around her were famous people, Lords and Ladies, soldiers and trumpeters!

"I can't see me yet," Ben said hoarsely.

"Nor me!" said Shani. "Oh, please, telly, *please!*"

Now the Queen was getting ready to make a speech.

"The bouquet!" Shani said between clenched teeth. "She's got to be given a bouquet!"

"The page-boy!" Ben gritted. "Surely she's got to have a page!"

Then – "There's me!" squeaked Shani.

"And me!" shouted Ben.

And it was true, they *were* there, on the TV screen. But only for a second. Only as a sort of mistake. Their faces filled the screen for a moment: then were gone. It happened again later on. But the faces did not say anything. They did not even move.

Soon after, the trumpeters blew a fanfare and the Queen drove off, waving, in an open carriage; and the Royal Occasion was over. An announcer's smiling face filled the screen. "We must apologize," she said, "for two small interruptions to that programme, caused by a technical fault."

When she said this, Shani burst into tears. "I wanted to be the bouquet girl," she sobbed, "and I end up as a technical fault!"

"And me – I was just a small interruption!" Ben said. "Grrrr!"

The TV set saw Shani crying and was deeply ashamed. "Pull yourself together!" it said. "Sort out those circuits! Get those poor children on television as S*T*A*R*S!!"

It couldn't manage to get them into a peakview programme.

But at last, because it was cleverer than any other telly, it came up with the right and clever answer! . . .

# Chapter Six

It was a Saturday – and the sports programmes were on – and there was to be *wrestling!*

"Great, brill!" said Ben, blopping the Blopper.

"You and your wrestling," Shani sniffed – but then the wrestling started.

"And now, grappling fans," said the presenter, "we give you –

"The Master of Mayhem!
The Mightiest Meanie!
The Beastliest Baddie!
None other than –
MURDEROUS MICK
McGURK!"

Mick McGurk strode through the crowd. Two old ladies hit him with umbrellas, but that could not hurt Mick McGurk! He was built like a gorilla.

He was as tough as an army tank.

"Ooo, isn't he awful!" Shani said, hugging herself.

"Let's hear a big welcome," the presenter continued, "for Mick McGurk's two opponents! Yes, folks, *two!* Mick's taking on *two* opponents at once!"

"I'd hate to be them, whoever they are!" Ben whispered.

"Me too!" Shani said. Then, "I can't see *us* anywhere. Can you?"

"Here they come, folks!" cried the presenter. "Mick McGurk's two brave opponents! Two new stars of the ring, never before seen on television!"

Two weeny little wrestlers, smothered in bright dressing gowns, crept under the ropes and into the ring.

"Give them a great big hand!" shouted the presenter. "Let's hear it for . . .

THE TERRIBLE TINIES!

SHANI AND BEN!"

"Oh no, please not!" cried Shani. "It can't be!"

"It is," Ben groaned. "The Terrible Tinies are *us!*"

## Chapter Seven

It was dreadful in the ring from the very beginning.

Mick McGurk shook hands with Shani and Ben and it was like having your hand run over by a steamroller.

He bounced up and down and said "GRRRARGH!" and the lights flickered.

It was even worse when the bell rang for round one. Murderous Mick McGurk advanced on Ben and Shani like a walking tower block.

He was huge! And hairy! And horrid!

"Let's run away!" Ben said.

"We can't!" Shani said. "Don't you see – at last, we're really here! Starring on TV!"

So they had to wrestle Mick McGurk. Or rather, Mick McGurk wrestled *them*.

First, he head-locked them.

Then he half-Nelsoned them.

Then he posted them.

Then he body-slammed them.

Finally he sat on them, making horrible noises and grinning at the crowd.

"He'll kill us!" moaned Shani.

"Just hope he does it quickly!" gasped Ben.

When the bell rang, Ben and Shani had to carry each other to their corner.

"We can't go another round, he's murdering us!" said Ben.

Shani could only answer "Ooo!" and "Ow!" and "Ouch!"

But suddenly she stopped groaning and said, "Wait! I've got an idea!"

She whispered in Ben's ear. He nodded his head. The bell went for the second round.

"I've never seen anything like it!" the TV man shouted into his microphone. "Mick McGurk is *running away!*"

"Yes! It's true!" he went on. "He's running away! And the Terrible Tinies are chasing after him, trying to catch him!"

Then – "They've caught him! They're all over him! They've got him on the canvas! They're on top of him! The crowd's going mad! And – folks, I can't believe my own eyes – Mick McGurk is begging for mercy! He's actually *crying!*"

In the ring, Mick McGurk roared, "I SUBMIT!" and banged the canvas with the flat of his enormous hand. "I give in!" he blubbered. "Make them stop! I can't take any more! Submit, submit, SUBMIT!"

The referee raised Shani's and Ben's hands over their heads and shouted, "THE WINNERS!"

## Chapter Eight

And then it was all over. Ben rubbed his bruises and said, "Wow! Agony!"

But Shani, who was just as bruised as Ben, said, "Whoopee! We did it! Now we're truly stars! All thanks to me!"

"Yes, that was a good idea of yours," Ben admitted.

"It was brilliant," Shani said. "But then, lots of big men are like Mick McGurk. I know my father is. And with *two* of us doing it –"

"Against two of us, he didn't have a chance!" Ben said. He admired his biceps in the mirror. His biceps were the size of walnuts. He raised an eyebrow and smiled a manly smile.

The fight was over and Murderous Mick McGurk was weeping like a baby. "Not fair!" he bellowed. "They're rotten cheats! And how did they discover my secret weakness? How did they guess that *I can't stand being tickled?*"

Next day, Ben and Shani settled themselves down on the carpet in front of the telly.

"Here's your orange drink – ouch!" Ben said to Shani. Even bending down to hand her the glass made him hurt.

"And your cake," he said. She reached up for it and said, "Thank you – ouch!" She too ached everywhere.

They settled themselves on the carpet in front of the TV. "Anything you want to watch?" Ben said.

Shani said, "No, I don't think so. I've had enough TV for the time being. Quite enough."

"Me too!" said Ben. And he filled his mouth with such a huge piece of cake that he went cross-eyed.

"Well! There's gratitude for you!" the TV said to itself, crossly. "After all I've done for them! But then, I'll never understand these humans . . ."